A PICTORIAL V
FROM THE
BEAR SHO
AT INDIANAPO

A PICTORIAL VIEW FROM THE BEAR SHOPS AT INDIANAPOLIS

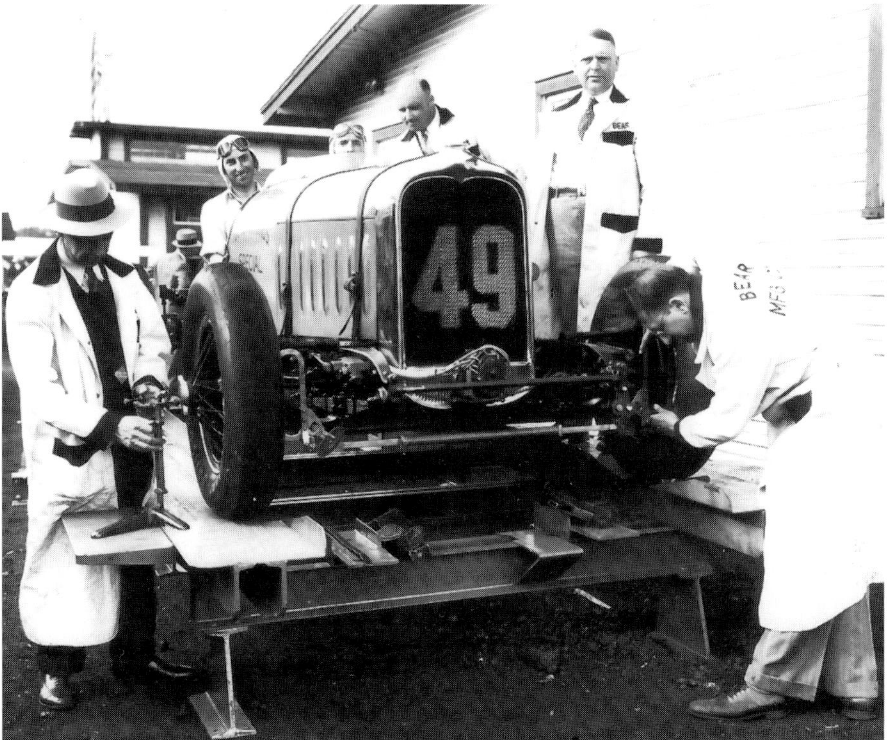

BY

RICHARD J. IVERSON

A PICTORIAL VIEW FROM THE BEAR SHOPS AT INDIANAPOLIS

Published by

Pitstop Books
P.O. Box 130
Zionsville, Indiana 46077

(317) 873-5507

Email: info@pitstopbooks.com
Website: www.pitstopbooks.com

ISBN-10: 0-9742668-2-5

ISBN-13: 978-0-9742668-2-4

First Printing: November 2006

Manufactured in the United States of America

Photos from Richard J. Iverson's Collection

Dedication

**To my old time racing buddies –
you know who you are.**

Special Dedication

**Ken "Moe" Moore
1933 – 2005**

BEAR
Comfort-Ride
WHEEL BALANCING
SERVICE

Table of Contents

BEAR
SAFETY SERVICE

Introduction

The Motivation:

The motivation and idea for this pictorial came about one afternoon in late December 2003. I was at a local outlet for a national bookstore chain having a discussion with the manager. I was lamenting the fact that his chain inventoried very few books on Indianapolis style auto racing. His comment was, "If there are not enough for you why don't you write one."

I made my point that it was not a case of books not on the market, I could name quite a few in print, but just not available through his store.

My next comment was, "I could possibly come up with enough material from my Indy memorabilia collection to do just that."

After giving this a thought over the next day I decided, WHY NOT! This pictorial is the result of that decision.

TO THE BEAR MFG. CO:

WE APPRECIATE YOUR BEAR SERVICE AT THE 1948 INDIANAPOLIS "500" RACE.

Ted Horn
Mauri Rose
Jimmy Jackson
Russ Snowberger
Louis Unser.
Billy DeVore
Floyd E. Davis
Sam Hanks
Al Miller
Mack Hellings.
Rex Mays
Hal Cole
Bennett Bros
Leo Bennett
Doc Williams
Joe Fagiol
Stanley Swindling
M L Ward
Lewis Welch -
Mike Salay
Tony Bettenhausen.

Joie Chitwood
Bill Holland
Duke Nalon
Wild Bill Cantrell
Chet Miller
Cliff Bergere
Lou Moore
Lee Wallard
Les Anderson
Harry McQuinn
Johnny "Mauro"
Lou Durant
Emil Andres
Walt Brown
Charles Van Acker
Milt Marion
Louis Bromme
Ken Fowler
Robt. C. Dietrich
Spider Webb.
Mel Hansen.

Paul Russo
Lyle M. Christie
Hal Robson
Bill Sheffler
Duane Carter
Johnny Mantz
Joe Lencki
Milt Fankhauser
Tom Hinnershitz
Louie Tomei
George Connor
Freddie Agabashian
Bud Winfield
Jack McGrath

Bear Company History

The Bear Manufacturing Company was founded by brothers Will Dammann and Henry Dammann. Initially the brothers developed and marketed a starter for the Ford Model T in 1913. After Ford developed their own electric starter, the Dammann brothers looked for other fields.

Will Dammann's ability to design and create tools and equipment spurred them to enter the wheel alignment service. He developed the first gauge to accurately measure the toe-in and camber of an automobile wheel assembly.

Bear was officially incorporated in 1917 in Rock Island, Illinois.

Eventually Will Dammann guided the company in designing gauges to measure all five of the basic alignment angles, frame straightening machines for automobile and truck frames. This equipment was followed by wheel balancing machines, brake service equipment, vehicle safety inspection lanes. This was followed over the years by automotive diagnostic equipment and diagnostic test lanes.

Bear maintained a complete Training Center in Rock Island, Illinois for automobile alignment body and frame straightening, wheel balancing, wheel and tire truers, brake and steering and diagnostic test lane.

Beginning in 1930, the Bear firm was involved at the Indianapolis Motor Speedway for the famous Indy 500 Mile race. During practice for the race, Will Dammann aligned race car front ends using hand held alignment gauges. This service was so well accepted, he returned in 1931 with a complete rack and equipment set-up. From then on for close to 70 years, Bear was noted as the Official Alignment Service of the "500".

Over the years Bear improved their facilities and services at the track. As race cars changed so did the equipment and services provided. From a rack outside in the weather to several improved garage buildings. A canvas tent for balancing operations to single garage bays. In the 1960s, Bear built a large three-bay service garage containing two-frame and alignment racks, with a bay for three to five wheel balancers.

1930s

The Bear Manufacturing Company's first alignment rack set up at the Indianapolis Motor Speedway was in 1931. Mr. Will Dammann, the Bear Company founder and president, is shown standing behind the right front wheel in the above picture. The car was the Butcher Brothers Special #49 and was entered and driven by Harry Butcher. A Buick chassis was powered by a Buick eight-cylinder. Butcher qualified 33rd at 99.343 m.p.h. and finished 38th. He completed only six laps as he was eliminated by a wreck in turn four.

1933 – RUSSELL “8” SPECIAL #4

Entered and driven by Russ Snowberger. A Snowberger chassis powered by a Studebaker eight-cylinder. Snowberger qualified 17th at 110.769 m.ph. and finished eighth. He completed all 200 laps at 99.011 m.p.h.

Bear technicians hard at work on Russ Snowberger’s car in 1933.

1936 – RING FREE SPECIAL #8

Entered and driven by Louie Meyer. A Stevens chassis powered by a Miller four-cylinder. He qualified 28th at a speed of 114.171 m.p.h. He finished first at an average speed of 109.069 m.p.h.

Louie Meyer stands by his Ring Free Special as the Bear technicians do a final alignment check on race day. Their work helped the car to finish the race in Victory Lane.

1936

ELGIN PISTON PIN SPECIAL #14

(On the alignment rack) The car was entered by Elgin Piston Pin Company. A Miller chassis powered by a Brisko four-cylinder. Frank Brisco qualified 20th at 114.213 m.p.h. Brisko finished 20th after running out of fuel on the 180th lap.

BOYLE PRODUCTS SPECIAL #53

(On the ramp) Entered by Boyle Motor Products and driven by Zeke Meyer. A Cooper chassis powered by a Studebaker eight-cylinder. He qualified 32nd at 111.476 m.p.h. and finished ninth completing 200 laps at a speed of 101.331 m.p.h.

1936 - HAMILTON-HARRIS SPECIAL #7

Entered by Williams S. White and driven by Shorty Cantlon. A Weil chassis powered by a Miller four-cylinder. He qualified 10th at 116.912 m.p.h. and finished 14th after running out of fuel on lap 194.

1936 – SUPERIOR TRAILER SPECIAL #54

Entered by Race Car Corporation and driven by Doc Williams. A Cooper chassis was powered by a Miller four-cylinder. Williams qualified 23rd at 112.837 m.p.h. and finished 16th, after running out of fuel on lap 192.

1937 – BURD PISTON RING SPECIAL #1

Entered by Lou Moore and driven by Mauri Rose. A Offy four-cylinder powered this Miller chassis. Rose qualified eighth at 118.540 m.p.h. and finished 18th after completing 127 laps. A broken oil line put the car out of the race.

1937 – SHAW-GILMORE SPECIAL #6

Entered and driven by Wilbur Shaw. A Offy four-cylinder powered this Shaw chassis. Shaw qualified second at 122.791 m.p.h. The Indiana native finished first with an average speed 113.580 m.p.h. This was Shaw's first Indy win.

1937 – HAMILTON-HARRIS SPECIAL #8

Entered by Louie Meyer, seen walking behind the car. This Stevens chassis was powered by a Offy four-cylinder. Ralph Hepburn qualified sixth at 118.809 m.p.h. and finished second with an average speed 113.565 m.p.h. Hepburn was only 2.16 seconds behind winner, Wilbur Shaw.

1937 – R.S. SPECIAL #12

Entered and driven by Russ Snowberger. A supercharged Packard 8-cylinder powered this Snowberger chassis. He qualified 30th at 117.353 m.p.h. and finished 27th after completing 66 laps. Clutch problems put the car out of the race. Johnny Seymour was relief driver during the race.

1937 – TOPPING SPECIAL #15

Entered by Henry J. Topping, Jr. A Supercharged Maserati 8-cylinder engine powered this Maserati chassis. Driven by Babe Stapp who qualified 31st at 117.226 m.p.h. He finished 31st, after completing 36 laps. Clutch problems put the car out of the race.

1938 BURD PISTON SPECIAL #23

Entered by Lou Moore. This Wetteroth chassis was powered by a 4-cylinder Miller. Driver Floyd Roberts sitting in car qualified first at 125.681 m.p.h. and finished first averaging 117.200 for the 500 miles.

1939 – BOYLE SPECIAL #2

Entered by Boyle Racing Headquarters. A Maserati supercharged eight-cylinder was the power in a Maserati chassis. Wilbur Shaw sitting on car side, qualified third at 128.977 m.p.h. and finished first averaging 115.035 m.p.h. This was Shaw's second win.

1939 – THORNE ENGINEERING SPECIAL #10

Entered by Joel Thorne, Inc. An Adams chassis was powered by a Sparks 6-cylinder. Driver Jimmy Snyder, sitting on car side qualified 1st at 130.138 m.p.h. and finished 2nd. He completed the 200 laps at a speed of 114.245 m.p.h.

1939 – BURD PISTON RING SPECIAL #51

Entered by Joe Lencki. A Lencki chassis was powered by a Lencki 6-cylinder. Tony Willman qualified 26th at 122.771 m.p.h. and finished 14th. Tony completed 188 laps and was eliminated by fuel pump failure.

Bear Wheel Balancing Shop shown in the late 1930s. Bear founder Will Dammann is shown on the far right with the Bear crew members.

Vintage 1933, Bear alignment rack at Indy was also used for passenger cars. Most likely this car was owned by an official.

1930s – Did You Know?

In 1931, Dave Evans drove the Cummins Diesel Special #8 nonstop to a 13th place finish.

# # # #

In 1935, the first engine bearing the Offenhauser name was in the winning car, Gilmore Speedway Special #5, driven by Kelly Petillo. Fred Offenhauser built the original Miller engines for Fred Miller from the 1920s. Offenhauser saved the engine program after Miller's bankruptcy in 1933.

# # # #

In 1935, crash helmets were required for the Indy 500.

# # # #

In 1935, green and yellow traffic lights were installed around the two and a half-mile track to keep driver informed of track conditions.

# # # #

In 1936, Louie Meyer became the first three-time Indy winner. He won the race in 1928, 1933 and again in 1936.

# # # #

In 1936, Indy was made safer when the inside walls were removed to provide the drivers more room so save the car. Also, the outside walls were made stronger and tilted inward to make it harder for cars to vault over them.

# # # #

In 1937, the short chutes were paved with asphalt. Only the front and back stretch were covered with the original bricks.

# # # #

In 1939, Louie Meyer wrecked his car on lap 198. While flying through the air as he was thrown out of the car he made a decision. He said, "That's it. I'm all done!" Meyer said, "I'm probably the only guy who retired from racing in mid-air."

1940s

Bear Company begin the 1940s as a fixture at Indianapolis. Shown above is the Indiana Fur Special #35 entered by Indiana Fur Company in 1940. The Wetteroth chassis was powered by an Offenhauser. Kelly Petillo qualified 13th at 125.331 m.p.h. and finished 21st. Petillo completed 128 laps and was eliminated by a rear main failure.

1940 – NOC-OUT HOSE SPECIAL #5

Entered by Lou Moore, Inc. Offenhauser powered this Wetteroth chassis. Cliff Bergere consulting with the Bear technician, qualified sixth at 123.673 m.p.h. and finished 27th. He completed 51 laps and was eliminated by an oil line problem.

1940 – MARKS SPECIAL #21

Entered by Joseph Marks. Offenhauser powered this Silnes chassis. Duke Nalon sitting in the car qualified 25th at 121.790 m.p.h. and finished 22nd. He completed 120 laps and was eliminated by a connecting rod failure.

1940 – ALFA ROMEO SPECIAL #34

Entered by Wharton-Dewart Racing. A supercharged Alfa Romeo 8-cylinder was the power in this Alfa Romeo type 8C-308 chassis. Chet Miller qualified 27th at 121.392 m.p.h. finished 17th after being flagged after 189 laps.

1941 – BOYLE SPECIAL #2

Entered by Boyle Racing Headquarters. A Maserati chassis had Maserati power. Driver Wilbur Shaw sitting in the car qualified third at 127.836 m.p.h. and finished 18th. Shaw only completed 151 laps and was eliminated by an accident in turn one. A wheel was marked as being bad but during the early morning garage fire at Indy on race day, the markings had washed off. Shaw was leading the race when the wheel collapsed and caused the car to crash. Shaw's attempt to win three races in a row came to an end.

1941 – AIR LINES SANDWICH SPECIAL #22

Entered and driven by Kelly Petillo. Offenhauser powered this Wetteroth chassis. Petillo qualified 19th at 124.417 m.p.h. and finished 27th. He completed only 48 laps and was eliminated by a connecting rod failure.

1941 – OFFUTT SPECIAL #12

Entered by Eddie Offutt. A Miller 6-cylinder powered this Miller chassis. Al Miller qualified 14th at 123.478 m.p.h. and finished 28th after completing 22 laps. Transmission failure eliminated Harry Miller's unique attempt to build rear-engine cars.

1946 – BOXAR TOOL & MFG. CO. SPECIAL #15

Entered by Joseph Hosso. Brisko 6-cylinder powered this Stevens chassis. Louis Tomei qualified 22nd at 119.193 m.p.h. and finished 26th. Tomei completed 34 laps and was eliminated by a oil line problem.

1946 – BOWES SEAL FAST SPECIAL #1

Entered by Bowes Racing, Inc. A supercharged Winfield 8-cylinder powered this Stevens chassis. Rex Mays qualified 14th at 126.861 m.p.h. and finished 30th after completing 26 laps. Mays was eliminated by a cracked manifold.

The Bowes Seal Fast car of Rex Mays, sets high and dry on the Bear alignment rack waiting for a dry track. It never rains at Indy in May!

1946 - THORNE ENGINEERING SPECIAL #16

Entered by Thorne Engineering Corp. A supercharged Sparks-6 was the power in this Adams chassis. George Robson qualified 15th at 125.541 m.p.h. and finished first averaging 114.820 m.p.h for the 500 miles.

1946 – SCHOOF SPECIAL #17

Entered by William Schoof. This Wetteroth chassis was powered by a Offy. Billy DeVore qualified 31st at 119.876 m.p.h. and finished 10th after spinning in the southwest (1st) turn on lap 167.

1946 – ELGIN PISTON PIN SPECIAL #18

Entered by Frank Brisko. A Maserati chassis was powered with a supercharged Maserati-8. Emil Andres qualified 11th at 121.139 m.p.h. and finished fourth at an average speed of 108.902 m.p.h. for the 500 miles.

1946 – OFFENHAUSER SPECIAL #28

Entered by Jimmy Chai. Offy powered this Wetteroth chassis. Driver Steve Truchan failed to qualify for the race.

1946 – ALFA ROMEO SPECIAL #33

Entered by Milt Marion. A supercharged Alfa Romeo 8-cylinder was the power in this Alfa Romeo chassis. Louis Durant qualified sixth at 118.973 m.p.h. and finished sixth averaging 105.073 m.p.h. for the 500 miles.

1946 – WALSH OFFENHAUSER SPECIAL #38

Entered by Ed Walsh. This Kurtis chassis had Offy power. George Connor qualified 30th at 120.006 m.p.h. and finished 24th after having piston failure after 38 laps. Connor's friend Henry Banks is standing by the car.

1946 – JACK MAURER SPECIAL #39

Entered by and driven by Bill Sheffler. Offy power was in this Bromme chassis. Sheffler qualified 25th at 120.611 m.p.h. and finished ninth being flagged after 139 laps.

1946 – OFFENHAUSER SPECIAL #41

Entered by Ross Page. A supercharged Duray-4 power was in this Kurtis chassis. Mel Hansen qualified 27th at 121.431 m.p.h. and finished 11th breaking a crankshaft on the 144th lap.

1946 – BRISTOW-MCMANUS SPECIAL #42

Entered by Robert J. McManus. A supercharged Miller 8-cylinder powered this Wetteroth chassis. Tony Bettenhausen qualified 26th at 123.094 m.p.h. and finished 20th after going out with a broken connecting rod on lap 47.

1946 – DON LEE SPECIAL #47

Entered by Don Lee, Inc. A supercharged Alfa Romeo 8-cylinder powered this Alfa Romeo chassis. Hal Cole qualified fourth at 120.728 m.p.h. and finished 32nd being stopped by a fuel leak on the 16th lap.

1946 – PHILLIPS MILLER SPECIAL #48

Entered by Overton A. Phillips. A Miller 8-cylinder powered this Bugatti chassis. Hal Robson qualified 23rd at 121.466 m.p.h. and finished 25th with a broken connecting rod on lap 37.

1946 – TALBOT SPECIAL #49

Entered by Zora Arkus-Duntov. Talbot six-cylinder power was in this Talbot chassis. Driver Arkus-Duntov failed to qualify for the race.

1946 – GREENE-HOLLAND SPECIAL #56

Entered by D. Greene and L. Holland. A six-cylinder Plymouth power was tried but driver Bruce Denslow failed to qualify.

1946 – LAGONDA SPECIAL #57

Entered and driven by Robert Arbuthnot. Lagonda 12-cylinder power was in this Lagonda chassis. Arbuthnot failed to qualify.

1946 – GRANCOR V-8 SPECIAL # 59

Entered by Grancor, Inc. (Granatelli Brothers). Ford V-8 power was in this Miller-Ford chassis. Danny Kladis qualified 33rd at 118.890 m.p.h. and finished 21st. On lap 46 the car developed fuel problems on the backstretch and was towed to the pits. The car was later disqualified for being towed.

1946 – JACKSON SPECIAL #61

Entered and driven by Jimmy Jackson. Offy power was in this Miller chassis. Jackson qualified fifth at 120.257 m.p.h. and finished second running the 500 miles at an average of 114.498 m.p.h.

1946 – SINGER SPECIAL #62

Entered and driven by Charles VanAcker. Voelker power was in this Steven chassis. VanAcker qualified at 115.666 m.p.h. Too slow for the starting field but was second alternate.

1946 – H-3 SPECIAL #64

Entered by Charles J. Hughes. Offy power was in this Miller-Ford chassis. Shorty Cantlon, standing by the rear tire, qualified 20th at 122.432 m.p.h. and finished 28th after suffering clutch failure on lap 28.

1946 – OFFENHAUSER SPECIAL #67

Entered by George Robson and C. Holland. Offy power was in this Ketteroth chassis. Driver A. Brummeier failed to qualify.

1947 – BOWES SEAL FAST SPECIAL #9

Entered by Bowes Racing, Inc. A supercharged Winfield-8 power in this Kurtis chassis. Rex Mays qualified 20th at 124.412 m.p.h. and finished sixth completing the 500 miles at an average speed of 111.056 m.p.h. Shown with front axle being aligned.

1947 – BLUE CROWN SPARK PLUG SPECIAL #16

Entered by Lou Moore. Offy power was in this Deidt chassis. Bill Holland qualified eighth at 128.755 m.p.h. which was the fastest time for the field. Holland finished second to his team mate Mauri Rose after receiving "E-Z" sign from car owner Moore.

1947 – BOGGS SPECIAL #23

Entered and driven by Tommy Boggs. Offy power was in this Cooper chassis. Boggs tried but failed to qualify the car for the race. Driver Louis Durant also tried but failed to qualify.

1947 – BLUE CROWN SPARK PLUG SPECIAL #27

Entered by Lou Moore. Offy power was in this Deidt chassis. Mauri Rose qualified third at 124.040 m.p.h. and finished first after passing team mate Bill Holland on lap 193. Rose's average speed for the 500 miles was 116.338 m.p.h.

1947 – PRESTON TUCKER PARTNER SPECIAL #44

Entered by Joe Lencki. This Stevens chassis was powered by a Lencki-4. Charles Van Acker qualified 24th at 121.049 m.p.h. and finished 29th after colliding with Paul Russo in the northwest (4th) turn on lap 24.

1947 – DON LEE MERCEDES SPECIAL #46

Entered by Don Lee, Inc. Mercedes chassis was powered by a supercharged Mercedes 12-cylinder. Duke Nalon qualified 18th at 128.082 m.p.h. and finished 16th after blowing a piston on lap 119.

1947 – DON LEE ALFA ROMEO SPECIAL #47

Entered by Don Lee, Inc. Alfa Romeo chassis was powered by a supercharged Alfa Romeo 8-cylinder. Ken Fowler qualified ninth at 123.423 m.p.h. and finished 15th after breaking an axle on lap 121.

1947 – JACK MAURER'S CLUB SOUTHERN SPECIAL #53

Entered and driven by Milt Fankhouser. Offy was the power in the Stevens chassis. Fankhouser qualified 11th at 119.932 m.p.h. and finished 30th after stalling in the southeast (2nd) turn on lap 16.

1947 – NOVI GOVERNOR MOBIL SPECIAL #54

Entered by W. C. Winfield. A supercharged Novi 8-cylinder power was in this Kurtis chassis. Herb Ardinger qualified fourth at 120.733 m.p.h. finished fourth at an average speed of 113.404 m.p.h.

1947 – KENNEDY TANK SPECIAL #58

Entered and driven by Les Anderson. Offy was the power in this Maserati chassis. Anderson qualified seventh at 118.425 m.p.h. and finished 11th after being flagged after completing 131 laps.

1948 – BELANGER MOTORS SPECIAL #16

Entered by Murrell Belanger. Offy was power in this Wetteroth chassis. Duane Carter qualified 29th at 126.015 m.p.h. and finished 22nd after losing a wheel and spinning in the southeast (2nd) turn on lap 59.

1948 – FANKHOUSER SPECIAL #23

Entered and driven by Milt Fankhouser. Offy was the power. Fankhouser failed to qualify for the race.

1948 – FEDERAL ENGINEERING SPECIAL #25

Entered by R. A. Cott. Maserati was the power in this Maserati chassis. Paul Russo qualified 25th at 122.595 m.p.h. and finished 32nd after developing an oil leak after 7 laps.

1948 – FEDERAL ENGINEERING SPECIAL #38

Entered by R.A. Cott. A Offy power in a Miller chassis. Driver Henry Banks watching his car being aligned. Banks failed to qualify the car for the race.

1948 – CITY OF TACOMA SPECIAL #63

Entered and driven by Hal Cole. Offy was the power in this Kurtis KK2000 chassis. Cole qualified 14th at 124.391 m.p.h. and finished sixth at the average speed 111.587 m.p.h. for the 500 miles.

1948 – PALMER CONSTRUCTION SPECIAL #64

Entered by Palmer Racing, Inc. An Adams chassis was powered by a Offy powered. Hal Robson qualified 18th at 122.796 m.p.h. and finished 15th after suffering valve problems after 164 laps.

1948 – SCHOOF SPECIAL #78

Entered by William Schoof. Offy powered this Wetteroth chassis. No driver was assigned and no qualification was attempted.

1948 – IDDINGS SPECIAL #91

Entered by John Iddings. Offy was the power in this Meyer chassis. Lee Wallard qualified 28th at 128.420 m.p.h. and finished seventh at an average speed of 109.177 m.p.h.

1949 – SHEFFLER OFFY SPECIAL #4

Entered and driven by Bill Sheffler. Offy was the power in this Bromme chassis. Sheffler qualified 22nd at 128.521 m.p.h. and finished 17th with a broken connecting rod on lap 160.

1949 – I.R.C. MASERATI SPECIAL #6

Entered by Indianapolis Race Cars, Inc. A supercharged Maserati 8-cylinder was the power in this Maserati chassis. Lee Wallard qualified 20th at 128.912 m.p.h. and finished 23rd with gear problem on lap 55.

1949 – DON LEE SPECIAL #8

Entered by Don Lee Motors, Corp. Offy powered this Kurtis KK2000 chassis. Mack Hellings qualified 14th at 128.260 m.p.h. and finished 16th after having valve troubles after 172 laps.

1949 – GRANCOR SPECIAL #14

Entered by Grancor Auto Specialists. Offy was the power in this Kurtis KK2000 chassis. Hal Cole qualified 11th at 127.168 m.p.h. and finished 19th after suffering a rod bearing insert problem on lap 117.

1949 – BELANGER SPECIAL #17

Entered by Murrell Belanger. This Stevens chassis was powered by a Offy. Duane Carter qualified fifth at 128.233 m.p.h. and finished 14th after having steering problems which caused a spin in the northeast (3rd) turn on lap 182.

1949 – SHEFFLER OFFY SPECIAL #52

Entered by Bill Sheffler. Offy powered this Bromme chassis. Manny Ayulo qualified 33rd at 125.799 m.p.h. and finished 28th with a broken connecting rod on lap 24.

1949 – NOVI MOBIL SPECIAL #54

Entered by W. C. Winfield. A supercharged Novi 8-cylinder powered this Kurtis chassis. Duke Nalon qualified first at 123.939 m.p.h. and finished 29th. Nalon lost a rear axle, crashed and burned in the northeast (3rd) turn on lap 23 while leading the race.

1949 – HOWARD KECK SPECIAL #61

Entered by Howard Keck Co. Offy power was in this Deidt chassis. Jimmy Jackson qualified seventh at 128.023 m.p.h. and finished sixth. Jackson went the full 500 miles non-stop at an average speed of 117.870 m.p.h.

1949 – PEUGOT SPECIAL #66

Entered and driven by Lindley Bothwell. Peugot chassis was powered by a four-cylinder Peugot. Bothwell failed to qualify.

1949 – WYNN'S OIL SPECIAL #69

Entered and driven by Bayless Levrett. Offy was the power in this Kurtis KK2000 chassis. Levrett qualified 29th at 129.236 m.p.h. and finished 24th after losing an oil drain plug on lap 52.

1949 – KARL HALL SPECIAL #73

Entered by Karl Hall. Offy was the power. Milt Fankhouser failed to qualify. Driver Manny Ayulo ran 120.490 m.p.h. also, too slow to qualify for the race.

1949 – THORNE ENGINEERING SPECIAL #81

Entered and driven by Joel Thorne. A six-cylinder Sparks was the power in this Mercedes-Benz chassis. Thorne failed to qualify.

BEAR CREW outside of Balancing Shop – Vintage 1940s

BEAR ALIGNMENT SHOP – Vintage 1940s

1940s – Did You Know?

The back stretch was paved with asphalt for the 1940 race.

# # # #

Wilbur Shaw became the second three-time Indy 500 winner in 1940. Shaw won in 1937, 1939 and 1940.

# # # #

In 1941 an early morning fire in the garage area destroyed several cars. One qualified car was the Offutt rear engine Miller driven by George Barringer. It had qualified in 15th position.

# # # #

Sam Hanks qualified the TOM JOYCE SPECIAL #28, a Offy powered Kurtis chassis in 27th position in 1941. Hanks crashed the day before the race and could not start on race day. This car was the first of many Kurtis designed and built race cars at Indy.

# # # #

In November 1945, Tony Hulman, at the urging of Wilbur Shaw, purchased the Indianapolis Motor Speedway. This action saved the track from becoming a housing development. The facilities were in sad condition after being idle during World War II. Shaw was named General Manager and President of the Speedway.

# # # #

Paul Russo drove the FAGEOL TWIN COACH SPECIAL #10 in the 1946 Indy 500. This car had two supercharged Offy midget engines; one in the front driving the rear wheels and one in the rear driving the front wheels.

# # # #

In 1947, Billy DeVore drove the PAT CLANCY SPECIAL #19 to a 12th place finish. This Offy powered Kurtis had two midget rear axles in tandem for a total of four driven rear wheels.

# # # #

Mauri Rose joined Louis Meyer and Wilbur Shaw as a three-time Indy 500 winner in 1948. Rose was co-winner with Floyd Davis in 1941, then won the 1947 and 1948 races.

# # # #

WFBM-TV in Indianapolis televised the 1949 Indy 500 to about 15,000 people viewing on 3,000 television sets.

1950s

All teams relied on Bear Company for expert service by the 1950s. In 1950 a dapper looking Johnnie Parsons poses by his Wynn's Friction Proof Special #1 on the alignment rack. The car was entered by Kurtis-Kraft, Inc. This Kurtis chassis was powered by an Offy. Parsons qualified fifth at 132.044 m.p.h and finished first, winning a rain-shortened "500". Parsons' crew discovered a cracked engine block on the morning of the race. The strategy for the race was to charge hard and collect as much lap prize money as possible before the engine blew. But the engine held until the race was stopped after 345 miles and Parsons was out front.

1954 – JIM ROBBINS SPECIAL #24

Entered by Jim Robbins Co. Offy powered this Stevens chassis. Cal Niday qualified 13th at 139.828 m.p.h. and finished 10th finishing all 200 laps at 126.895 m.p.h.

1954 – MCNAMARA SPECIAL #83

Entered by Lee Elkins. Offy powered Kurtis/Wetteroth chassis. Eddie Johnson qualified at 137.599 m.p.h. which was too slow for the race. Johnson was first alternate.

1954 – SCHMIDT SPECIAL #88

Entered by Peter Schmidt. Offy powered a Kuzma chassis. Manny Ayulo qualified 22nd at 138.164 m.p.h. and finished 13th, flagged after completing 197 laps.

1955 – HINKLE SPECIAL #3

Entered by Jack B. Hinkle. This Kurtis chassis was powered by a Offy. Jack McGrath qualified third at 142.580 m.ph. and finished 26th after having magneto problems after 54 laps.

1955 – MALLOY SPECIAL #5

Entered by Emmett J. Malloy. Offy was the power for this Pankratz chassis. Jimmy Reece qualified 15th at 139.991 m.p.h. and finished 33rd. A broken connecting rod caused a spin in southwest (first) turn on lap 10.

1955 – WALSH SPECIAL #9 (#91)

Entered by Ed Walsh as car #91 for Spider Webb. This was a Offy powered Kurtis KK4000 dirt car. As far as we know the car never made any practice laps. The team was concentrating their efforts on their Kurtis KK500C #9 Indy roadster which failed to qualify for the race.

1955 – D-A LUBRICANTS SPECIAL #22

Entered by Racing Associates. Offy power was in this Kurtis KK500B chassis. Cal Niday qualified ninth at 140.302 m.p.h. and finished 16th. Niday crashed and was seriously injured in the northwest (4) turn on lap 170.

1955 – JIM ROBBINS SPECIAL #23

Entered by Jim Robbins. A Stevens chassis was Offy powered. Jerry Hoyt qualified first at 140.045 m.p.h. and finished 31st after an oil leak on lap 40.

1955 – CRAWFORD SPECIAL #49

Entered and driven by Ray Crawford. Offy powered this Kurtis KK500B chassis. Crawford qualified 23rd at 139.206 m.p.h. and finished 23rd after having valve problems on lap 111.

1955 – ANSTAD ROTARY SPECIAL #64

Entered by Rotary Engineering Co. Offy was the power in this Kurtis chassis. Driver LeRoy Warriner failed to qualify.

1955 – MARTIN BROS. SPECIAL #71

Entered by T. W. Martin and W. T. Martin. Offy was the power in this Kurtis chassis. Al Herman qualified 16th at 139.811 m.p.h. and finished seventh. Herman was named Rookie-of-the-Year.

1955 – MCNAMARA SPECIAL #73

Entered by Kalamazoo Sports, Inc. This Kurtis chassis had Offy power. Driver Len Duncan failed to qualify after having a wreck in practice.

1955 – LEITENBERGER SPECIAL #76

Entered by F. L. Leitenberger. Offy powered this Pawl chassis. Johnny Kay qualified at 132.193 m.p.h. which was too slow for the race.

1955 – MERZ ENGINEERING SPECIAL #77

Entered by Merz Engineering, Inc. Offy power was in a Kurtis KK500C chassis. Walt Faulkner qualified seventh at 139.762 m.p.h. and finished fifth after completing 200 laps averaging 125.377 m.p.h.

1956 – FEDERAL ENGINEERING SPECIAL #42

Entered by Federal Automotive Associates. This Kurtis KK500C chassis was powered by an Offy. Fred Agabashian qualified seventh at 144.069 m.p.h. and finished 12th flagged after 196 laps.

1957 – CHAPMAN SPECIAL #43

Entered by H. A. Chapman. Offy powered this Kurtis KK500G chassis. Eddie Johnson qualified 20th at 140.171 m.p.h. and finished 25th with wheel bearing failure on lap 93.

1957 – MCNAMARA SPECIAL #83

Entered by Kalamazoo Sports, Inc. A Kurtis KK500C chassis was powered by an Offy. Ed Elisian qualified seventh at 141.777 m.p.h. and finished 29th after having a timing gear failure on lap 51.

1958 – JONES & MALEY SPECIAL #33

Entered by Cars, Inc. Offy power was in this Epperly chassis. Tony Bettenhausen qualified ninth at 143.919 m.p.h. and finished fourth averaging 132.855 m.p.h. for the 500 miles.

1958 – BARDAHL SPECIAL #52

Entered by Pat Clancy. Offy power was in this Kurtis KK500G-2 chassis. Al Keller qualified 21st at 142.931 m.p.h. and finished 11th averaging 128.498 m.p.h for the race.

1958 – NOVI AUTO AIR CONDITIONING SPECIAL #54

Entered by Novi Racing Corp., Inc. Supercharged Novi power was in this Kurtis chassis. Bill Cheesebourg qualified 33rd at 142.546 m.p.h. and finished 10th avoiding the serious crash on the first lap. Cheesebourg average for the 500 miles was 129.149 m.p.h.

1958 – SCLAVI & AMOS SPECIAL #55

Entered by Fred Sclavi. Offy power was in this Kurtis/Kuzma chassis. Driver Eddie Russo failed to qualify.

1958 – HELSE SPECIAL #57

Entered by H. H. Johnson. Offy power was in this Kuzma chassis. Art Bisch qualified 28th at 142.631. m.p.h. and finished 33rd after being involved in the first lap crash.

1958 – BRYANT HEATING & COOLING SPECIAL #61

Entered by J. S. Donaldson. Offy power was in this Kurtis KK500G chassis. Eddie Johnson qualified 26th at 142.670 m.p.h. and finished ninth completing all 200 laps with an average speed of 130.156 m.p.h.

1958 – SAFETY AUTO GLASS SPECIAL #95

Entered by James E. Shreve. This Kurtis chassis was powered by an Offy. Drivers LeRoy Warriner and Bill Homier were unable to qualify the car.

1959 – EL DORADO ITALIA SPECIAL #12

Entered by Scuderia El Dorado. Maserati eight-cylinder power was in this Maserati chassis. Ralph Liguori qualified at 136.395 m.p.h which was too slow to make the starting field.

1959 – PETER SCHMIDT SPECIAL #44

Entered by Peter Schmidt. A Kuzma chassis was powered by an Offy. Eddie Sachs qualified second at 145.425 m.p.h. and finished 17th after having a gear tower bolt problem on lap 182.

Bear Wheel Balancing Tent. Shown early 1950 vintage.

New Alignment Rack being installed in the Bear Wheel Alignment Shop. Vintage 1954 (Foster)

1950s – Did You Know?

Following a serious crash during the 1951 Indy 500, three-time winner Mauri Rose retired from racing.

# # # #

When Troy Ruttman won the 1952 Indy 500 in the Agajanian #98, he was only 22 years old, becoming the youngest winner ever.

# # # #

Art Cross, who finished fifth in the 1952 Indy 500 driving the BOWES SEAL FAST SPECIAL #33, was named the first ever Rookie-of-the-Year.

# # # #

Duke Nalon qualified the NOVI GOVERNOR SPECIAL #9 in 26th position and finished 11th in the 1953 Indy 500. This was the last front wheel drive car to run in the Indy 500.

# # # #

In 1956, the United States Auto Club replaced the American Automobile Association as the sanctioning body for the Indianapolis 500.

# # # #

The new Indianapolis Speedway Office and Museum were opened at the 16th Street and Georgetown Road entrance in 1956.

# # # #

The historic Wooden Pagoda observation building was replaced by a new modern Control Tower in 1957.

# # # #

Sam Hanks, the 1957 Indy 500 winner, announced his retirement from racing, after a 23-year career, in Victory Lane.

# # # #

Roll bars and fireproof uniforms were made mandatory for the 1959 Indy 500.

1960s

1961 – BRYANT HEATING & COOLING SPECIAL #8

Entered by Pete Salemi and Rick Rini. Offy was the power in this Watson chassis. Len Sutton qualified eighth at 145.897 m.p.h. and finished 19th after suffering clutch failure after 110 laps. Actor Jim Davis of TV show "Rescue 8" shown visiting Bear Shop.

1960 – GREENMAN-CASALE SPECIAL #24

Entered by Lysle Greenman. Offy power was in this Kuzma chassis. Driver Johnnie Tolan failed to qualify.

1961 – COOPER-CLIMAX SPECIAL #17

Entered by Cooper Car Co., Ltd. Climax four-cylinder power was in this Cooper chassis. Jack Brabham qualified 13th at 145.144 m.p.h. and finished ninth averaging 134.116 m.p.h. for the 500 miles. Brabham made a good showing with his under-powered rear-engine Climax. This was the beginning of the end for the front-engine roadster.

1961 - FEDERAL ENGINEERING SPECIAL #34

Entered by Federal Automotive Associates. Offy powered this Kurtis KK500E chassis. Norm Hall qualified 32nd at 144.555 m.p.h. and finished 10th averaging 134.104 m.p.h. for the 500 miles.

1961 - DENVER-CHICAGO TRUCKING SPECIAL #62

Entered by Myron Osborn. This Watson chassis was powered by an Offy. Driver Chuck Arnold failed to complete qualifying run.

1962 – DEAN-AUTOLITE SPECIAL #2

Entered by Dean Van Lines, Racing Division. Offy was the power in this Ewing chassis. Eddie Sachs qualified 27th at 146.431 m.p.h. and finished third with an average speed of 140.075 m.p.h. for the 500 miles.

1962 – J. H. ROSE TRUCK LINE SPECIAL #27

Entered by Bob Phillips. Offy powered this Lesovsky chassis. Don Davis qualified 12th at 147.209 m.p.h. and finished fourth averaging 139.768 m.p.h. for the 500 miles.

1963 – BRYANT HEATING & COOLING SPECIAL #9

Entered by D. V. S., Inc. Offy was the power in this Watson chassis. Eddie Sachs qualified 10th at 149.570 m.p.h. and finished 17th after losing a wheel, spinning and crashing in the northeast (3) turn on lap 182.

1963 – DEAN VAN LINES SPECIAL #10

Entered by Dean Van Lines. This was a Ewing chassis powered by an Offy. Chuck Hulse qualified 11th at 149.340 m.p.h. and finished eighth at an average speed of 140.064 m.p.h. for the 500 miles. Shown here using the drive-over toe alignment gauge.

1963 – WYNN'S FRICTION PROOFING SPECIAL #25

Entered by Joseph B. Hunt. Offy was the power in this Watson chassis. Driven by Jimmy Daywalt and Chuck Rodee, both failing to complete qualifying runs.

1963 – BMC ASTON-MARTIN SPECIAL #48

Entered by Kjell H. Qvale. Aston-Martin six-cylinder was the power in this Cooper chassis. Pedro Rodriquez qualified at 146.687 m.p.h. but the speed was too slow to make the race.

1963 – HARVEY ALUMINUM SPECIAL #81

Entered by Mickey Thompson. Chevy V-8 was the power in this Thompson chassis. Maston Gregory qualified at 147.517 m.p.h. but the speed was too slow to make the race.

1963 – THOMPSON HARVEY ALUMINUM SPECIAL #84

Entered by Mickey Thompson. Chevy V-8 was the power in this Thompson chassis. Al Miller qualified 31st at 149.613 m.p.h. and finished ninth averaging 139.524 m.p.h. for the 500 miles.

1964 – SHERATON-THOMPSON SPECIAL #1

Entered by Ansted-Thompson Racing. Offy was the power in this Watson chassis. A. J. Foyt, Jr. qualified fifth at 154.672 m.p.h. and finished first for Foyt's second 500 victory. Foyt averaged 147.350 for the 500 miles. This was the last win for the reliable "Roadster".

1964 – VITA FRESH ORANGE JUICE SPECIAL #8

Entered by Gordon Van Liew. Offy power was in this Edmonds chassis. Driver Dempsey Wilson wrecked trying to qualify.

1964 – ZINK-URSCHEL TRACKBURNER SPECIAL #52

Entered by Zink-Urschel, Slick, Inc. Offy power was in this Brabham chassis. Jack Brabham qualified 25th at 152.504 m.p.h. and finished 20th with a split fuel tank on lap 77.

This 1964 photo shows a typical day in the Bear Shop on any Time Trial weekend.

1964 – THOMPSON SEARS ALLSTATE SPECIAL #82

Entered by Mickey Thompson. Ford V-8 power was in this Thompson chassis. Maston Gregory qualified at 148.038 m.p.h. but was too slow for the starting field. Second alternate for the race.

1964 – AMERICAN RUBBER & PLASTICS SPECIAL #87

Entered by John Chalik. Offy power was in this Epperly chassis. Driver Chuck Rodee failed to qualify.

1965 – WYNN'S SPECIAL #4

Entered by Leader Cards, Inc. Ford power was in this Watson chassis. Don Branson qualified 18th at 155.501 m.p.h. and finished eighth after being flagged after 197 laps.

1965 – STP OIL TREATMENT SPECIAL #6

Entered by STP Division-Studebaker. Novi power was in this Granatelli chassis. Driver Bobby Unser wrecked during practice.

1965 – FEDERAL ENGINEERING SPECIAL #10

Entered by Federal Automotive Associates. Offy power in this Gerhardt chassis. Driver Bob Harkey failed to qualify.

1965 – ZINK-URSCHEL-SLICK TRACKBURNER SPECIAL #52

Entered by Zink, Urschel, Slick, Inc. A Brabham chassis powered by an Offy. Jim McElreath qualified 13th at 155.878 m.p.h. and finished 20th after leaving with rear end gear problems on lap 66.

1965 – VITA-FRESH ORANGE JUICE SPECIAL #44

Entered by Gordon Van Liew. Huffaker chassis powered by an Offy. Demsey Wilson drove the car but an accident in practice ended his hopes of making the race.

1965 – AGAJANIAN HURST SPECIAL #98

Entered by J. C. Agajanian. Ford was the power in this Kuzma-Lotus chassis. Parnelli Jones qualified fifth at 158.625 m.p.h. and finished second, averaging 149.200 m.p.h. for the 500 miles.

1966 – JIM ROBBINS SPECIAL #27

Entered by J. M. Robbins. Ford power was in this Vollstedt chassis. Billy Foster qualified 12th at 149.490 m.p.h. and finished 24th. Foster wrecked on the first lap after being squeezed into the outside wall. The accident on the front straight eliminated 11 cars. Graham Hill in the foreground was just looking around.

1966 – RACING ASSOCIATES SPECIAL #39

Entered by Herb Porter. A turbocharged Offy power was in this Watson chassis. Bobby Grim qualified 31st at 158.367 m.p.h. and finished 31st after being involved in the first lap crash that eliminated 11 cars.

1966 – VALVOLINE SPECIAL #53

Entered by Vatis Enterprises, Inc. Offy power was in this Huffaker chassis. Gary Congdon qualified 16th at 158.688 m.p.h. and finished 25th after being wrecked in the first lap crash.

1966 – VALVOLINE II SPECIAL #54

Entered by Vatis Enterprises, Inc. Offy power was in this Huffaker chassis. Eddie Johnson qualified 29th at 158.898 m.p.h. and finished seventh after stalling on lap 175.

1966 – HARRISON SPECIAL #93

Entered by J. Frank Harrison. Chevy V-8 power in this Eisert chassis. No driver assigned and the car failed to qualify.

1966 – AGAJANIAN'S REV 500 SPECIAL #98

Entered by J. C. Agajanian. Offy power in this Shrike (made by Halibrand) chassis. Parnelli Jones qualified fourth at 162.484 m.p.h. and finished 14th after suffering a wheel bearing failure on lap 87.

1967 – STP OIL TREATMENT SPECIAL #40

Entered by STP Division of Studebaker Corp. Pratt & Whitney Turbine powered this Granatelli chassis. Parnelli Jones qualified sixth at 166.075 m.p.h. and finished sixth, after being forced out on lap 196 with a gear box failure.

Side view of the STP Turbine car on the Bear rack. Parnelli Jones led 171 laps of the race. Failure of a $6.00 bearing halted his run for the win.

Rear view of the STP Turbine #40. This is the view most of the competition saw during the race.

1967 – COMPTON SPECIAL #44

Entered by Richard Compton. Offy was the power in this Vollstedt chassis. Driven by Ronnie Duman and Chuck Arnold. Neither driver was able to qualify the car.

1967 – MICHNER PETROLEUM SPECIAL #60

Entered by Michner Petroleum, Inc. Ford powered this Gerhardt chassis. Driver Mickey Shaw failed to qualify.

1967 – ASHLAND OIL COMPANY SPECIAL #75

Entered by A. B. C. Engine, Inc. Ford was the power in this Lotus chassis. Driven by Ronnie Bucknam and Maston Gregory. Neither driver was able to qualify this car.

1968 – RETZLOFF CHEMICAL SPECIAL #5

Entered by Retzloff Racing Team. Ford was the power in this Lola chassis. Driven by Carl Williams. The car failed to qualify and was wrecked in practice while being driven by Al Unser.

1968 – QUAKER STATE SPECIAL #14

Entered by Caves Buick Co. Offy was the power in this Gerhardt chassis. Driven by Chuck Hulse and failed to qualify. The car was wrecked in practice.

1968 – MICHNER PETROLEUM SPECIAL #22

Entered by Michner Petroleum, Inc. Ford powered this Eagle chassis. Bill Cheesebourg qualified at 157.274 m.p.h. but was too slow to make the starting field.

1968 – STP OIL TREATMENT SPECIAL #30

Entered by STP Corp. Turbine powered the Lotus chassis. Driver Mike Spence crashed in southwest (1st) turn during practice. Spence was fatally injured.

1968 SPEEDY BROASTED CHICKEN SPECIAL #34

Entered by Frank Fiore. Chevy powered this Huffaker chassis. Driven by Chuck Booth and Dee Jones but neither driver was able to qualify the car.

1968 – JACK ADAMS AIRCRAFT SPECIAL #36

Entered by Jack Adams. Ford power was in this Lola chassis. Driven by USAC sprint car ace Larry Dickson, who qualified at 159.652 m.p.h. Too slow to make the starting field.

1968 – NAVARRO INJECTION SPECIAL #50

Entered by Barney Navarro. Rambler 6 was the power in this Watson chassis. Driven by Les Scott, who didn't finish his driver's test, and Jerry Titus, who wrecked in practice.

1968 – CLEAVER-BROOKS SPECIAL #59

Entered by Hayhoe Racing Enterprises. Turbocharged Offy powered this Brabham chassis. Ronnie Duman qualified 26th at 162.338 m.p.h. and finished sixth after being flagged at 199 laps.

1968 – SHELBY RACING SPECIAL #69

Entered by Carroll Shelby. General Electric Turbine powered this Wallis chassis. Driven by Dennis Hulme and the car was withdrawn without attempting to qualify.

1968 – GREER SPECIAL #82

Entered by James Greer and A. J. Foyt, Jr. (shown behind car) Ford power was in this Coyote chassis. Jim McElreath qualified 13th at 165.327 m.p.h. and finished 14th after 179 laps when engine stalled and would not restart.

1968 – VALVOLINE SPECIAL #94

Entered by Vatis Enterprises, Inc. Turbocharged Offy was the power in this Finley chassis. Sam Sessions qualified 31st at 162.118 m.p.h. and finished ninth after being flagged after 197 laps.

1969 – VALVOLINE SPECIAL #11

Entered by Vatis Enterprises, Inc. Turbocharged Offy was the power in this Finley chassis. Sam Sessions qualified 23rd at 165.434 m.p.h. finished 12th after being flagged after 163 laps.

1969 – BRYANT HEATING & COOLING SPECIAL #21

Entered by Vollstedt Enterprises, Inc. Turbocharged Ford powered this Vollstedt chassis. Larry Dickson qualified 31st at 163.014 m.p.h. and finished ninth after being flagged after 180 laps.

1969 – FEDERAL ENGINEERING SPECIAL #31

Entered by Federal Automotive Associates. Turbocharged Offy was the power in this Gerhardt chassis. Driven by Bobby Jones and failed to qualify.

1969 – NAVAROO ENGINEERING SPECIAL #50

Entered by Barney Navaroo. Rambler 6 was the power in this Watson chassis. Driver Les Scott wrecked trying to qualify.

1969 – MINNESOTA SERENDIPITY SPECIAL #51

Entered by Gavan, O'Reilly & DeMulling. Ford was the power in this Watson chassis. Driven by Cy Fairchild and Dee Jones. None of the drivers were able to qualify the car.

1969 – MAXSON SPECIAL #89

Entered by Darwin Maxson. Offy was the power in this Epperly chassis. This front engine roadster style car was driven by George Benson and Les Scott. Both drivers failed to complete a qualifying run.

A damaged roadster front axle being straightened on the rack in 1961.

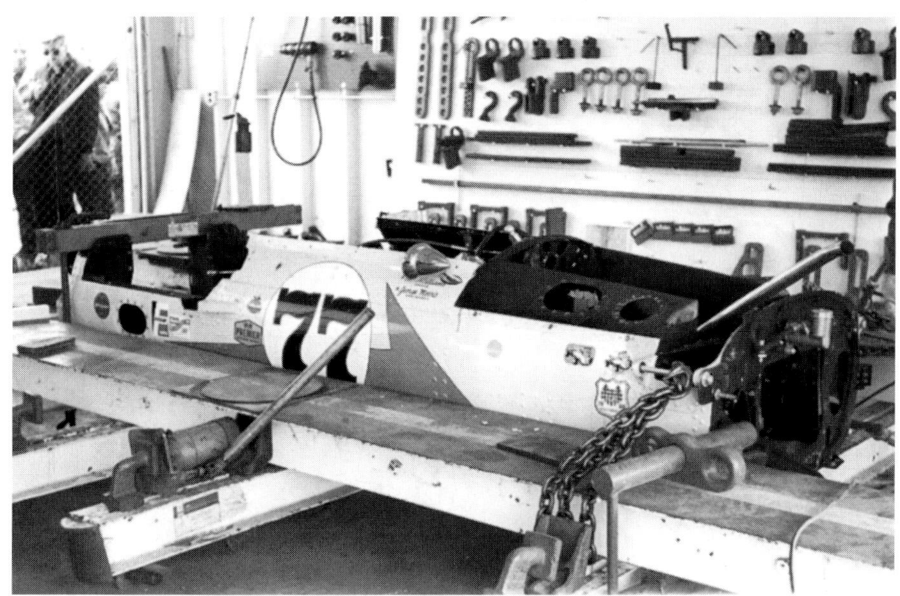

1966 – DAYTON STEEL WHEEL SPECIAL #77

Entered by George Walther. This Gerhardt chassis was powered by Ford. Carl Williams qualified 25th at 159.645 m.p.h. and finished 16th. After completing 38 laps a problem with an oil line put the car out of the race. Shown is the tub being straightened on the frame rack.

A completely stripped frame being straightened on the rack in 1962.

A rolling chassis being straightened in the rack by Dick Iverson in 1965.

Bear wheel balancing tent set-up for the Indy 500 in 1960.

More modern wheel balancing tent set-up for the 1962 Indy 500.

Much more improved and modern Bear wheel alignment frame and balancing shop built for the 1964 Indy 500.

Wheel balancing area of the new Bear shop for the 1964 Indy 500.

Bear crewman Dick Iverson is shown aligning the Ford Mustang Pace Car in 1964. Before each race, Bear would make sure the Indy Pace Car was in perfect alignment.

1960s – Did You Know?

Rookie Jim Hurtubise set the one-lap speed record of 149.601 m.p.h. in 1960.

\#   #   #   #

In 1960, as the race cars made their practice lap, a homemade scaffold toppled in the northwest turn. Two spectators were killed with another 40 injured.

\#   #   #   #

The total prize purse in 1960 was $369,150 with the winner receiving $110,000. By comparison, the 1911 total purse was $27,000 with the winner getting $14,000.

\#   #   #   #

John Zink entered a Brabham chassis with a mid-engine 375 HP Boeing turbine in 1962 but it failed to qualify.

\#   #   #   #

In 1967, Parnelli Jones led 171 laps only to have a $6.00 bearing fail with 4 laps left in the race. Jones was driving the STP #40 turbine powered car for Andy Granatelli, nicknamed "Silent Sam" or as the press called it, "WHOOSHMOBILE".

\#   #   #   #

In 1967 there were a record 90 entries for the Indy 500 race.

1970s

Bear Crew Chief, Dick Iverson showing the newly designed and installed alignment racks to USAC Technical Committee Chairman Frank DelRoy and key members of his staff. The racks, specially designed for race car front and rear alignment were installed before the 1971 Indy 500.

1970 – CANAL 9 BUENOS-AIRES SPECIAL #8

Entered by Agajanian-Fass Racers. Offy powered this Mongoose chassis. Driven by Carlos Alberti Pairetti and Larry Dickson. Failed to qualify.

1970 – BRYANT HEATING & COOLING SPECIAL #21

Entered by Vollstedt Enterprises, Inc. Ford power was in this Vollstedt chassis. Driven by John Cannon. Failed to complete qualifying run.

1970 – INDY ON A SHOESTRING SPECIAL #26

Entered by Indy on a Shoestring, Inc. Offy powered. Driven by Al Loquasto. Failed to qualify.

1970 – STEARNS MANUFACTURING SPECIAL #31

Entered by Federal Automotive Associates. Turbocharged Offy power was in this Gerhardt chassis. Jim Malloy qualified ninth at 167.895 m.p.h. and finished 33rd after breaking a radius rod and hit the front stretch wall coming for the green flag.

1970 - MIDWEST MANUFACTURING COMPANY SPECIAL #34

Entered by Carl Gehlhausen. A Huffaker chassis powered by a V-8 Chevy. Driver Tom Bigelow failed to qualify.

1970 – GIFFORD SPECIAL #71

Entered by Lloyd W. Gifford. Chevy powered this Gerhardt chassis. Driven by Bruce Jacobi. Failed to qualify.

1970 – WYNN'S SPITFIRE 98 SPECIAL #98

Entered by Agajanian-Fass Racers, Inc. Mongoose chassis was powered by a turbocharged Offy. Driver Denny Zimmerman failed to qualify.

1971 – TRAVELODGE SLEEPER SPECIAL #10

Entered by Dick Simon, Ltd. A turbocharged Ford power was in a Lola chassis. Dick Simon qualified at 168.903 m.p.h. but was too slow to make the starting field.

1971 – TRAVELODGE SLEEPER SPECIAL #10

Entered and driven by Dick Simon. Ford powered a Lola chassis. Failed to qualify. Simon then entered the race in 33rd position after replacing team driver John Mahler in the #44 car.

1971 – INDY ON A SHOESTRING SPECIAL #26

Entered by Indy on a Shoestring, Inc. Ford powered a Gerhardt chassis. Driven by Al Loquasto. Failed to qualify after wrecking in the southwest turn.

1971 – STP GAS TREATMENT SPECIAL #20

Entered by STP Corporation. Turbocharged Ford power in this McNamara chassis. Steve Krisiloff qualified 27th at 169.835 m.p.h. and finished 31st with an oil leak causing a spin in the northeast (3) turn on lap 10.

1971 – INDY ON A SHOESTRING SPECIAL #26

Entered by Indy on a Shoestring, Inc. Ford powered this Gerhardt chassis. Driver Al Loquasto failed to qualify after wrecking in the southwest turn.

1971 – TRAVELON TRAILER SPECIAL #65

Entered by Ernest Ruiz. Offy powered this Gerhardt chassis. Driven by Jigger Sirois and Arnie Knepper. Failed to qualify.

1971 – JERRY GRANT SPECIAL #78

Entered by Jerry Grant Racing Ent. Offy powered this Eagle chassis. Driven by Sam Posey. Failed to qualify.

1971 – NORRIS INDUSTRIES SPECIAL #92

Entered by Shelby-Dowd Performance. Turbocharged Ford powered this Eagle chassis. Jerry Grant qualified at 168.492 m.p.h. but was too slow for the starting field.

WYNN'S KWIK-KOOL SPECIAL #98

Entered by Agajanian-Fass Racers. Turbocharged Ford power was in a Lola chassis. Sam Sessions qualified 25th at 170.358 m.p.h. finished 27th with engine failure at lap 43

1972 – AMERICAN MARINE UNDERWRITERS SPECIAL #14

Entered by Lindsey Hopkins. This was an Antares chassis with an turbocharged Foyt power. Roger McCluskey qualified 20th at 182.676 m.p.h. and finished 24th after dropping out with a burned valve on lap 92.

1972 – BRYANT HEATING & COOLING SPECIAL #17

Entered by Vollstedt Enterprises. Offy power in a Vollstedt chassis. Denny Zimmerman qualified 28th at 180.027 m.p.h. finished 19th after suffering a broken distributor on lap 116.

1972 - STP DOUBLE FILTER SPECIAL #20

Entered by STP Corporation. Foyt powered a Lola chassis. Driven by Bob Harkey. Failed to qualify.

1972 - CAVES BUICK SPECIAL #37

Entered by Caves Buick Co. Offy power in a Gerhardt chassis. Lee Kunzman qualified 30th at 179.265 m.p.h. and finished 17th, spinning after losing a tire on lap 131.

1972 – TRAVELODGE SLEEPER SPECIAL #44

Entered by Dick Simon, Ltd. Turbocharged-Foyt power in a Lola chassis. Dick Simon qualified 23rd at 180.424 m.p.h. and finished 13th after being flagged after 186 laps.

1972 – STEED OIL SPECIAL #91

Entered by Frank Curtis. Turbocharged-Offy powered this Curtis chassis. Driven by Bill Puterbaugh. Failed to qualify.

1973 – TRAVELODGE EAGLE SPECIAL #44

Entered by Dick Simon, Ltd. Turbocharged-Foyt power was in an Eagle chassis. Dick Simon qualified 27th at 191.276 m.p.h. and finished 14th with a broken piston on lap 100.

1973 – MILLER HIGH LIFE SPECIAL #56

Entered by Dick Hammon. Turbocharged-Foyt powered. Jim Hurtubise qualified at 184.237 m.p.h. but was too slow for the starting field.

1973 – MIDWEST-DURA-POT RACERS SPECIAL #58

Entered by Gehlhausen & Masson. A Finley chassis was powered by a turbocharged-Offy. Driven by Arnie Knepper who failed to take the flag for his qualifying attempt and by Johnny Parsons who wrecked in a practice run.

1973 – STP GAS TREATMENT SPECIAL #60

Entered by STP Corporation. Turbocharged Offy powered a Eagle chassis. Graham McRae qualified 13th at 192.031 m.p.h. and finished 16th, going out on lap 91 with a broken header.

1973 – CARLING BLACK LABEL SPECIAL #73

Entered by Roy Woods Racing. Turbocharged Offy powered a Eagle chassis. David Hobbs qualified 22nd at 189.454 m.p.h. and finished 11th in a rain-shortened race after completing 107 laps. The winner, Gordon Johncock, completed 133 laps.

1973 – UNSPONSORED CAR #89

Entered by Automotive Technology. A McLaren chassis powered by a turbocharged Offy. John Martin qualified 24th at 194.383 m.p.h. and finished eighth after being flagged after 124 laps.

Bear Racing Crew and Shop – 1970 vintage.

Dick Iverson shows former Indy driver Billy DeVore a promotional poster of a car he drove in the 1946 race. The car was the SCHOOF SPECIAL #17. He finished in 10th position. Vintage 1971.

1970s – DID YOU KNOW?

In 1971, the Dodge Pace car, driven by a local Indianapolis dealer, skidded out of control in pit lane and struck a photographers stand. In all 29 people were injured, two seriously.

# # # #

Bruce Walkup qualified for the 1970 race in a Mongoose chassis equipped with a roll cage.

# # # #

The inside and outside retaining walls were raised to a uniform 32 inches in 1974 as a safety precaution.

# # # #

Firestone Tires, which had won 43 Indy 500's, from 1920 through 1966, withdrew from racing in 1975.

# # # #

A. J. Foyt, Jr. won his 4th Indy 500 pole position in 1975, tying a record set by Rex Mays.

# # # #

The new Indy Hall of Fame Museum opened inside the main entrance in 1976.

# # # #

Red signal lights were installed around the perimeter as a safety measure for the 1976 race.

# # # #

Janet Guthrie averaged 188.403 MPH to become the first woman driver to qualify for the Indy 500 Race in 1977.

# # # #

In 1978, Tom Sneva became the fastest qualifier to date for the Indy 500. Sneva averaged 202.156 MPH for his 4-lap run.

# # # #

The 1979 Indy 500 had a record entry list of 103 cars.

Miscellaneous

1909 BUICK SPECIAL #10

Driven by Bob Burman. Won the first race run on the Indianapolis Track in 1909, a 250-mile event. Shown here in 1959 for a 50th Anniversary event. The car was driven by the 1925 Indy winner, Peter DePaolo, to officially open the qualifying trials.

A Plymouth stunt car from "Lucky Teter's World Champion Hell Drivers" show getting aligned on the Bear rack in 1937. Joie Chitwood eventually purchased the Teter equipment after Teter's death and started the "Joie Chitwood Thrill Show".

International Land Speed Record holder, Ab Jenkins (3rd from the right), poses with the Bear crew at Indy in 1938. The car is a one of a kind special bodied Duesenberg Sport Roadster. Notice the large "DUESENBERG" on the hood and visible on the cowl is Ab Jenkins.

The Bear crew with the 1912 Indy 500 winning car. The NATIONAL #8 was driven by Joe Dawson to first place after starting seventh position. The picture is 1937 vintage.

Deep in thought, Rex Mays was sitting by his car on the alignment rack. The car, the BOWES SEAL FAST SPECIAL #1 started in the 14th spot but only lasted 26 laps to finish 30th in 1946.

L. B. Arp, Bear VP with Jack McGrath the driver of the HINKLE SPECIAL #3 in 1955. McGrath started third and finished 26th with magneto failure on lap 54.

Actor Sebastian Cabot visits with Bear president Vic Day and crewman Marcel Periat at the Bear balancing shop, vintage 1956.

Sam Hanks, the 1957 Indy 500 winner shown being interviewed during May. Hanks drove the BELOND EXHAUST SPECIAL #9 (not on rack) to victory, then announced his retirement from racing while in Victory Lane.

Actor-comedian Morry Amsterdam visited with Bear crewman M. Dickerson and Bear president, Vic Day, at the Bear balancing shop in 1962.

Driver Tony Bettenhausen presented Bear president Vic Day with a helmet from the Indy drivers. Vintage 1960.

Mickey Thompson was explaining his HARVEY ALUMINUM SPECIAL #35 to USAC officials. The car was an Buick powered rear-engine, four-wheel independent suspension. Vintage 1962.

A. J. Foyt, Jr., driver of the SHERATON-THOMPSON SPECIAL #1 watching chassis inspection in 1965. Foyt finished 15th with rear end gear problems on lap 115.

Sportswriter John O'Donnell with Mario Andretti, driver of the DEAN VAN LINES SPECIAL #12 in 1965. Andretti finished third and was named Rookie of the Year.

Mechanic-builder, Louis Unser behind the ARCIERO BROTHERS SPECIAL #63 in 1965. Maserati powered an Archiero chassis. Driven by Al Unser failed to qualify.

Maserati engine was used in the Arciero Brothers Special #63.

Dick Iverson, Bear – Mel Kenyon – John O'Donnell – Red Haiston, Bear – outside the Bear Shop in 1965. Kenyon, driver of the FEDERAL ENGINEERING SPECIAL #27 was second alternate for the race.

Bob Williams, Bear – Parnelli Jones the driver of the STP Turbine #40 – Ed Butt, Bear – were discussing chassis set-up on the turbine car - 1967.

Bear president Vic Day (left) and Colin Chapman, (center) owner, designer and builder of Lotus Race Cars, shown visiting the Bear Shop in 1968.

Col. M. Dickerson and Bear crew chief Dick Iverson (seated in car) with the THORNE ENGINEERING Special #16. The car was driven by George Robson to victory in the 1946 Indy 500. Vintage 1969.

CUMMINS DIESEL SPECIAL #8 was driven by Dave Evans in 1931. Cummins power was in a Duesenberg chassis. Finished 13th as the car went non-stop for the 500 miles. Shown here on display in 1969.

The Bear race crew poses with 1972 Indy 500 winner Mark Donohue. Donohue had just presented them with a color picture of the 1971 front row at Indy. Vintage 1972

Frenchman Rene Thomas, the 1914 Indy winner, chats with Peter DePaolo, the 1925 Indy winner, in the Bear Shop. The car in the rear is the DeLage driven by Mr. Thomas in 1914. Vintage 1973.

Rene Thomas, winner of the Indy 500 in 1914, is shown here kissing the tire of the DeLage Special #16. He averaged 82.47 m.p.h. for the 200 laps. Mr. Thomas was visiting the race in 1973.

The engine of the 1914 DeLage Special on display on the Bear rack in 1973. The engine was a 4-cylinder with a 380 cubic inch displacement.

DeLage Special #16 was driven by Rene Thomas of France to victory in the 1914 Indy 500. The car is shown here on the Bear rack with Karl Kiser, IMS curator and Dick Iverson, Bear crew chief. Many times in May a noted car will be displayed in the Bear Shop during race weekend. In 1973, the year this car was shown, Rene Thomas was present at Indy for the race.

(Left to right) Dick Iverson, Billy Woodruff, A. J. Foyt, Jr. were discussing a Scholarship to the Bear Automotive School that was awarded to Woodruff in 1975.

ABOUT THE AUTHOR

My first recollection of Auto Racing goes back to 1940 when my family attended a Midget Auto Race in Muscatine, Iowa. That was my first taste that has lasted to this day. I still enjoy any form of open-wheel racing.

I became hooked on the Indianapolis 500 after attending the 1950 race with a high school friend whose father just happened to be the local representative of Bear Manufacturing Company here in Rock Island, Illinois. A week after graduating from high school, I enrolled in the Bear Safety Service School. I was hired at the school later that summer as an operator-instructor. This career decision lasted for a total of 50 years doing alignment, balancing, body frame, brake work, safety inspection and diagnostic work.

The best part of my work was continuing my presence at the Indy 500. I became a full-time member of the Bear Indy 500 race crew. This was like a seventh heaven for a race-car nut. I eventually became crew chief for the 500 operation. During this time I was fortunate to aid in establishing our shops at the the Ontario, California 500 and the Pocono, Pennsylvania 500. I was also

United States Auto Club

ıle USAC Indianapolis — 4910 West 16th Street, Speedway, Indiana 46224 — Phone (317) 244-7637

September 22, 1971

Mr. Richard Iverson
Bear Manufacturing Corporation
Rock Island, Illinois 61201

Dear Dick:

I have appointed you a member of our Championship Technical Committee and also a member of our National Technical Committee.

We are very pleased to be able to have your vast knowledge of chassis work and will now be side -by- side with a former fine "Bear Man" Marcel Pieriat, who has contributed a great deal towards improving the safety factor in our present race cars.

We will have our 1st meeting for 1972 sometime in March or April, and will let you know well in advance.

Thanking you for accepting a post on our Committee, and wishing you and Keith the best of everything, I remain,

Sincerely yours,

Frank Del Roy
Technical Supervisor

FD:siw

fortunate to be appointed to the USAC Championship Technical Committee and the USAC Technical Advisory Committee.

During the time I was working at Indy I began to amass many souvenirs. I began to get photos, press kits, arm bands, posters, spark plugs, wheels and tires and Indy 500 metal pit badges. My photo collection came from many sources – Racing friends and Bear

United States Auto Club

Cable USAC Indianapolis — 4910 West 16th Street, Speedway, Indiana 46224 — Phone (317) 244-7637

February 3, 1972

Mr. Dick Iverson
Bear Manufacturing
Rock Island, Illinois

Dear Mr. Iverson:

The United States Auto Club wishes to thank you and all the people who helped make 1971 our safest year in racing.

In keeping with USAC's policy to continue to improve our safety standards, we would be pleased if you would serve on our new Technical Advisory Committee for 1972.

The members are as follows:

Technical Chairman	Frank Del Roy
Medical and Safety	Dr. Thomas Hanna
State Fire Marshall	Harvey H. Hacker
Magnaflux Corporation	Ed Oclon
Firestone	Bob Cassaday
Goodyear	Bud Poorman
Bear Manufacturing	Dick Iverson
Premier Industrial	open
Safety	Harry Hartz
Metallurgical	S. A. Silbermann
Wheels	Ted Halibrand

Unless I hear from you to the contrary, this letter will serve as your appointment.

Sincerely,

Charlie

Charles T. Brockman
President

CTB:rp

cc: Richard King
Frank Del Roy

Public Relations to name a few. I also was given many early photos from Clyde Wills, an early Bear crewman. Some photos for this book were also borrowed from my long-time friends Ken and Bruce Moore. I hope that these photos are of interest to most open-wheel fans. I believe many will be seen in print for the first time.

Index

Car Index